INTIMATE GEOGRAPHY
POEMS
ISHMAEL VON HEIDRICK-BARNES

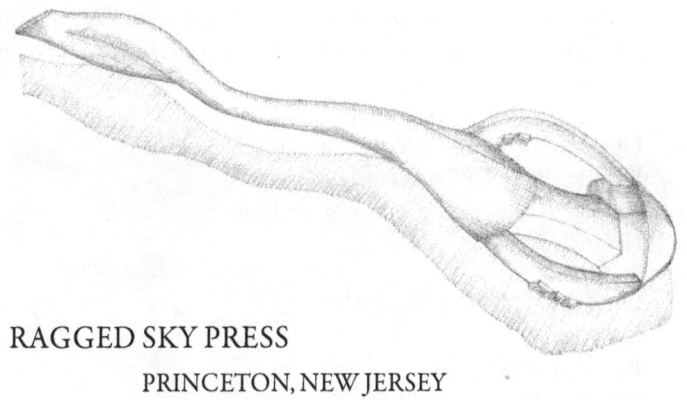

RAGGED SKY PRESS
PRINCETON, NEW JERSEY

INQUIRIES AND INFORMATION:
www.vonheidrickbarnes.com

COPYRIGHT © BY ISHMAEL VON HEIDRICK-BARNES
Published by Ragged Sky Press, PO Box 312, Annandale, NJ 08801
www.raggedsky.com

All rights reserved. No part of this book may be used or reproduced in any manner whatsoever without written permission, except in the case of quotes for personal use and brief quotations embodied in critical articles or reviews.

Library of Congress Cataloging-in-Publication Data
Heidrick-Barnes, Ishmael von, 1962-
  Intimate geography : poems / Ishmael von Heidrick-Barnes. -- 1st ed.
    p. cm.
  ISBN 978-1-933974-11-8 (pbk.)
  I. Title.
  PS3608.E36158 2012
  811'.6--dc23   2012016556

ART BY ROGER RIGORTH: www.roger-rigorth.de
BACK COVER PHOTO: MARGARETA HEIDRICK-BARNES

FIRST EDITION
PRINTED IN THE UNITED STATES OF AMERICA

CONTENTS

GEOMORPHOLOGY

Impostor	3
My Father's House	4
Aphasia	10
Craniotomy	11
Mastectomy	12
Portrait of a Surgeon in Free Verse	13
Hallucination Hawk	14
Post-Traumatic Stress Disorder	15
Cutter	16
Final Exit	17
Death Mask	18
Dying	19
Bread	20
Moving	21
The Dust Bowl	22
Mr. Watt's Garage	23
Barbershop	24
In the Flight Path	25
Garments	27
Proposal	28
Stay-at-Home Father	29
Word	30
Baby Buddha	31
Portrait of My Daughter	32
Darshan Dancer	33
Speechless	35
Changing Houses	36
Forgetting	37
One Heartbeat	38
Broken Earth	39
Answered Prayer	40

TOPOGRAPHIC PILGRIMAGES

Laika	43
Apollo	44
George Washington	46
Trenton, 2009	48
Flying over the Midwest	49
Dancing on the Charles Bridge	50
Hemingway's Suitcase	51
Zona Rojo	52
Falling	53
Skateboarding in Nuremberg	54
Sweet Destiny	55
Berlin, 1987	56
Savignyplatz (Berlin, 2007)	59
Potsdamer Platz Pigeons	60
Intimate Geography	61
Firenza	62

PERSONAL GEOGRAPHY

Prayer of Forgiveness	65
Gone	66
Rumi's Mirror	67
Mathematical Proof	68
Seven Caves	69
Silence	70
Projectile Point	71
Indian Rock	72
When Oceans Had Fish	73
Blue Screen	74
Doorways	75
X-Rays	76
Carving a Pumpkin	77
Transfiguration	78
Walking Close to Cliffs	79
Parrot Street	80
Construction Site	81

San Diego	82
Jesus Was a Woman	83
Incandescent	84
Floating	85
After the Witch Creek Fire	86
Wild	87

GEOPOLITICS

Butterfly Storm (*Vanessa Cardui*)	91
Canyon Sin Nombre	92
El Niño	93
Poetry for Crows	94
Walking through Dachau	95
Invasion	96
President Clinton's Cigar	97
Ground Zero	98
Koenig's Sphere	99
Dumbing Down	100
The Sixth Year	101
Flying Flags	102
The Assassination of Benazir Bhutto	103
Stauffenberg's Eye	104
The Eighth Year	105
Leading Economic Indicator	106
Seeing	107
Political Fetish	108
Boarding a Sinking Ship	110
Feast of Forgetting	111
Blood on Latex	113
Striking a Child	114
Accident Scene	115
WMD	116
Notes	118
Acknowledgments	119

FOR M²

"It is a way I have of driving off the spleen and regulating the circulation." —Herman Melville

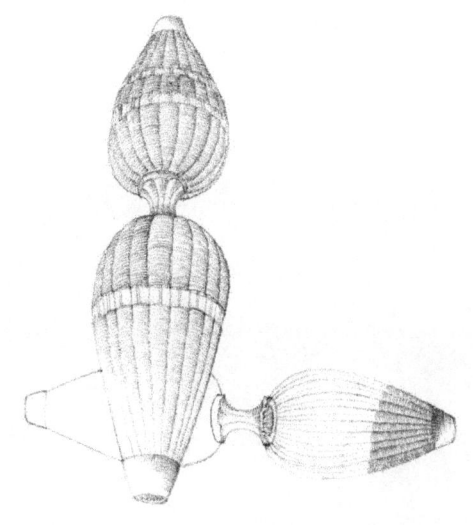

GEOMORPHOLOGY

IMPOSTOR

The gentleman
making small talk in my dinner jacket
is an impostor

One hand
welcomed him into your house
the other turned me
away

I say again:

The man sitting at your table
is a stranger

Hear me
when I tell you his mouth is a two-way mirror
and you like what you see

MY FATHER'S HOUSE
In memory of Billy Lynn Barnes 1934–1998

We come home to say goodbye—
but you have already gone

As if you just left for Yuma
in a caravan of Winnebagos
loaded with Coors beer and kielbasa
to watch the Padres' Spring training   or boarded a bus
full of senior citizens to Laughlin or Vegas
in search of the jackpot you never found

The house is safe
inside its coat of anonymous brown paint:

Immune to El Niño
and the subtle erosion of sun—
not a single smudge of earth staining white trim

The lawn
is an envious green I have not seen in years:

A still-life geometric equation
bordering the same cement driveway
you helped us summit as kids

A windowsill of rectangular hedges shrouding foundation
not one branch leaning against wall   not one leaf loitering in shade:

Just the fingerprints of your rake
retracing the upper mid-line incision
cut into your chest when I was seventeen

I pull back the black metal door:

A screen in an old confessional
and enter a living room of silk flowers and brown paneling

Oversized couches
gather around the oak tabernacle of a sleeping TV set
a gold clock with matching crucifix
count out each second
as if time were something that could be measured

Something of you
remains behind to greet me in each sibling's embrace
something betrayed by the absence of shadow   in the silence
necessitating word

I was born so that it might be spoken
I am alone because it hasn't been heard
I weep because it can only be found in the texture of tears

In the kitchen
surrounded by the twelve apostles
and Da Vinci's portrait of a Caucasian Christ
my mother incants tearful refrains
to Kansas   Colorado   North Carolina

In between conversations
with relatives she has neither seen nor liked in years
she sinks into my arms in search of an anastomosis
neither of us can crawl inside anymore
and that space between us   is the beginning of love

On top of the refrigerator
my father's heart medications await consecration:

Minute white hosts in amber monstrances
each container inscribed with Latin invocations
summoning catacombs of gods
crucified in the name of Jesus
sleeping beneath religion and science
announcing   *The hour of salvation is at hand*

Pull down the dead skin glove of my hand
and you will see that even in avulsion
life adheres to form:
nailed to the hallway
faces frozen into paper
outlast flesh and bone

I am afraid of the final two rooms
in this expanding universe of luminance and shade
each with its separate bed and coarctation of light

I fear the clothing
that hangs unwrinkled in my father's closet
the shoes shined
and assembled inside the boxes in which they were purchased

A waterfall of predictable ties
dripping down from aluminum racks
into shirts   socks   folded into drawers of dressers   quietly tucked
away

Afraid of what lies
in the satin lining of a sports coat
or the pockets of trousers   still wrapped in cellophane
from the dry cleaners

I wonder about objects
I cannot find:
lint that rolls up
into a chrysalis in fingers
slipping away with wind

I seek sanctuary
in my father's garage
in its cement floor stained by the tears of countless cars
this was his refuge   the eye of his storm

This is where he sat
drinking beer   dreaming lottery tickets   retirement
Olympic gold medals for his sons
where he sweated
shovels   hoes   paint cans   and boxes of Christmas decorations
every kind of tool imaginable to man

This is where he tried to teach me
about carburetors   timing   tune-ups   and fast breaks
on basketball courts
where he cut hair after twenty years of barbering
left him balding and grey

This is where he kicked my brother in the face and threatened to kill me
if I didn't move out of his way
this is where he met himself in me   refusing to leave:

The battered mother he tried to protect
the father he wanted to forget   the fist he became

This is where he confessed
to being a cheerleader in high school
after years of telling me John Wayne was his idea of a *real man*

This is where he hung awards for jobs well done
where his eyes drowned in the wound from which his anger came
yet never broke the surface of that stream

This is where he kept love letters to my mother for forty years
in an old bag marked   *U.S. Navy*
eventually throwing them away
afraid his kids might sift through the sediment of his heart

What about the rooms
he never knew existed?

The unfinished additions   motorhomes he wanted to buy
the country he never saw?

How can anyone calculate
the cost of not affording
the Grand Canyon   Wrigley Field
the old farm in Kansas where he spent summers as a child?

In the backyard
the jacaranda should be blooming
but my father has cut back
its branches   and resected the major arteries of its arms

I feel the phantom pain of lost limbs
still reaching out in purple celebration of sky
and I am grateful
that I grew enough to love you as you were   Daddy
not how I wanted you to be

Happy to walk here with you inside of me
unraveling the coiled garden hose
and tending to the lawn

APHASIA

He cannot hear the hands of her eyes
stroking sunlight from hair

Half a hemisphere
raining
roman numerals

One face
folded in black umbrella
the other:

Lacuna
streaking
white canvas

CRANIOTOMY

Lifting the scalp flap
onto a bed of moist sponges

Cutting between two points
drilled into skull with a rongeur

Sinking
a fragment of cranium into saline solution

Bone wax
applied to control bleeding

Peering into the patient's brain:

Dura mater pulsating with each heartbeat
synapses firing into unconscious thought

Mystery of matter and mind:

The cerebral circus contemplating itself

MASTECTOMY

I held the severed breast of a patient
in latex hands

Sunset-red areola
under the OR's adipose light

Feeling the weight of infants
nurtured by mother's milk   a lifetime of embraces
translated into the ambient memory of each cell

All these benign thoughts
sliding into a Ziploc bag   tagged
with name   number   bar code

Rushed to lab   dissected   discarded

PORTRAIT OF A SURGEON IN FREE VERSE

She works per diem   prefers a number 15 blade

Cannot close
until the final sponge count is complete

A sense of humor
sharper than a Gigli saw

She came out of anesthesia too soon

Gowned and gloved
the world beyond her sterile field:

Contagion

HALLUCINATION HAWK

The shrink
sitting on the ninth floor
scribbling EEGs onto prescription pads

Red-tailed hawk
never registering in the doctor's script
slamming head-on into windows hallucinating sky

POST-TRAUMATIC STRESS DISORDER

The already broken wave
at odd angle with sea

Drafting reckless lines:

White water swirling on blue slate

Millimeters before reason rushes into fibrillation
the magnetic pull of ocean calling it back into itself

What remains
meeting oncoming surf
thrusting its crest to new heights

CUTTER

On Ward B
Patient Y's excavations
uncovered the Etruscan figurine of a fertility goddess
buried beneath
three layers of skin

FINAL EXIT

Living in a room
spray-painted Spanish

Letters dripping
where poets paused
too long
between words

Visitors pissing:
plastic buckets   soiled clothing   24 hours of darkness
because the 60-watt bulbs have been stripped of filaments
blackened by Bic lighters:
crack pipes in an addict's artistic hands

She is proud of her scarred wrists:
the only windows left in hell

I leave while there is a razor blade of light framing her door

DEATH MASK

What frightens me about death
isn't dying

It's living on a stage
without atrophy's final exit

What frightens me about death
isn't dying

It's living among actors
omitting lines

What frightens me about death
isn't dying

It's the choreographed absence of loss:

A mask more grotesque than necrosis
because it buries us alive

DYING

I died today
please don't send flowers

It's a process every perennial is born to do

Someone called the time
I didn't have a watch

The palm I planted in 1999
continued growing

It's impossible to come to my senses

I can't complain

Some kind person removed the intubation tube
pulled the Foley catheter
washed my body with a sponge

It is
as it has to be:

Everything happening without reason
no defibrillating second thoughts just the continuous flat line—life

BREAD

Mother is breaking eggs

Albumen
surrendering yolk's sunny disk
stirred into milk   sugar

She can't keep the tears in her teaspoon eyes
from spilling
into bowl

Hands
white with sticky flour
she is kneading

Kneading
fists full of pastry on wooden board
punching it down
into greased pans
throwing old dishcloths over dough

Waiting
all afternoon for bread to rise

MOVING

Homeless
until opposing objects
rent wind's voice

Her mournful aria seeping into automobiles
through slivers in window frames

The bubble wrap percussion of rain
on safety glass:

Tears foreclosing eyes

Come morning
storm's map unfolded on the hood of car

THE DUST BOWL

Rain came late
to Dad's dust bowl eyes

I was ten years old
when he wept loaves of bread
for my grandfather who forced him to steal from stores

What
could a boy raised on TV dinners
say to the face of hunger?

MR. WATT'S GARAGE

Mr. Watt
never parked his car
inside the garage

A perpetual darkness
enveloping mountains of cardboard boxes

A blind catfish growing larger than its murky aquarium

BARBERSHOP

The barbershop's walls were mirrors
exposing angles of my father's face
I had not known before:

Razor
straight sideburns   flattops   five-o'clock shadow

After closing
sharpening blades with the leather strap
used to beat my brother

Leaving me
to push mounds of human hair with industrial sized brooms

IN THE FLIGHT PATH
Remembering PSA Flight 182

A wave of fog hangs over Point Loma
forcing aircraft
to eat Encanto sky

Growing up in the flight path
we laid on lawns
looking for crosses in clouds

Weekends
when money was tight
dad drove us out to tarmac
where pilots waved from cockpits before takeoff

727s taxied to the end of runway
radioing for clearance

We felt the thrust of jet engines
in abdomens

Watched the lightning descent of planes between buildings
driving with the wing of one arm
outside windows of a '67 Plymouth
flying home from school

In the Fall of 1978
when it rained fuselage over North Park
fire
burned through the houses of our childhood

I awoke
an amalgam of twisted metal and man

GARMENTS

I want to stand naked
in the churches

Give back
the garments of priesthood
torn from Christ's body

I want to know what it means
to forgive the man
whose kiss betrays me

I want to understand how it feels to be:

Woman

PROPOSAL

She was barefoot
when I asked her to marry me

Waves bending starlight into beach
the dress her grandmother danced in seamlessly sewn onto sand

My anonymous ally leaning over Hotel Del balcony
white dinner jacket hollering:

Better say yes to a fellow
willing to get down on his knees in this day and age

STAY-AT-HOME FATHER

Spending afternoons segregating laundry
tending to the tremors of machines

The difficult task beginning in silence:

Hanging
shirts   folding towels into thirds

Warm fabric remembering womb
static shock wrinkling sheets

The ritual reward of a full basket
all socks mated

WORD

At five a.m.
the word awakens in our daughter—
blue breast milk of vowels crawling without consonants
the cradle writers rock all their lives

Monosyllabic sunlight peeking through blinds
a mobile of moments toying sound

At five a.m.
the music box opens   a nursery of language sings—

The survival of species
contingent upon play

BABY BUDDHA

Baby Buddha
will not sleep outside her father's arms

A string of 108 tears
calling the parent to meditate upon his original face

Two hours
at one with rocking chair   Her Holiness   the Dalai Lama
chanting dream mantras into Daddy's ear

PORTRAIT OF MY DAUGHTER

Greta's Birth
Bundle of muscles
crying until she found consolation
wrapped in the blanket of her father's voice
love has no beginning

First Words
Momma
papa   dog-dog   duck
hi   moon
by   up
up a synonym for down

Greta's Hair
Strangers touch her hair
bestowing blessings
bands of gold
wrapping around fingers:
sunlight unraveling in their hands

First Work
Handing her father the sun on a sheet of paper—
overwhelming warmth!

Greta's Eyes
Night falls malignantly over moon:
eyelids unwrapping unbelievably blue worlds

Cyclops
Laughing nose to nose
marveling how two wide eyes
can appear as one

DARSHAN DANCER
For Linda Brown

Once by a pool
in the meditation gardens
while pointing to the yoga posture of koi
she confessed to being a go-go dancer in some past life

I wrote myself
out of a womb of comfortable bookshelves   Cabernet Sauvignon
into the courtyard left littered with leaves

She brought
Wordsworth   Forché
the shoes of Paramahansa Yogananda
tucked beneath the master's bed

She taught me
how to seduce women in French
walking across the Pont Mirabeau
without leaving Miracles Café

When I sank into ice caves of depression
she showed me how to strike out for the South Col
and when to descend

We went to galleries   salons
where poets paid homage
to the mother who had given birth to their art

She spoke of sonnets in free verse
offerings of sagebrush distilled into stanzas

When my father died
and I wrote for two weeks without stopping
she would not allow me to alter a single word

She knew laughter's lotus
floated in darshan tears

I saw her reflection
drifting within karmic wheels of water—

A light
sinking its arms into shadow
as if it were saying to all the world—

Shall we dance?

SPEECHLESS

Sending her trunks forward
when traveling abroad

Summiting the tallest peaks
on seven spiritual continents in high heels

Never leaving home without a spare pack of Gauloises
because   *You never know when Robert Redford might
round the corner to bum a cigarette*

Eyes lasered by moonlight
midnight telephone calls from the collective unconsciousness

Always one fender bender
from penthouse to asylum

Pagan poetess   goddess   actress
leaving the world speechless
taking her final cruise
on the most expensive day of the year to buy flowers

CHANGING HOUSES

Houses change as occupants grow older

Niches large enough to lose selves inside
become smaller

Cabinets closed by towering heights
inexplicably within reach

Walls organically contract   exhale

Floorboards buried beneath decades of carpet
resurface

Lamplight skips off sweat-polished wood
as if someone's father closed escrow yesterday
40 years of love breathing
windows   doors

FORGETTING

Enables mothers to have a second child
allows shipwrecked men to discover new worlds

Erodes walls
eats away fences
makes old enemies
new friends

Sheds tears magnifying stars invisible to naked eyes

Looks back from mountaintops
remembers magnificent views

ONE HEARTBEAT

The radial artery
pulsating within our handshake

The mass of his 87-year-old journey:
death of wife   children   cancer   four corners of color
balanced on beaded walking stick adorned with feathers

Can't you feel the sun dancing?   He asks   *Water blowing*
Wind dripping?

His fingers flapping into bluebird wings
We are all brothers   there are no differences
everything has one heartbeat   He sings
flying from the palm of my hand

BROKEN EARTH

Eight weeks out of jail
you walked upstairs and slammed yourself into the kingdom of God

The only words you left were letters from prison—

Stolen shards of scripture
the priest mouthed out loud at your funeral:

Holy water sprinkled on raging fire

The damage
could not be contained by prayer

It required four pallbearers to carry your coffin
the weight of your six-year-old daughter's tears
pulling us down
inside ourselves

I wanted to scream
into the deaf face of Jesus
rising from cross

Addiction is hypodermic
No man can wash his hands free of drugs!

After the church service
driving sheep to graveyard

White gloves
laid on the lid of your casket
mechanically lowered into broken earth

ANSWERED PRAYER

Paramedics found the alcoholic mother kneeling
against her unmade bed

Fingers interlocking eyes
in shame's final act of contrition

A multitude of shot-sized bottles
staggered throughout her motel room

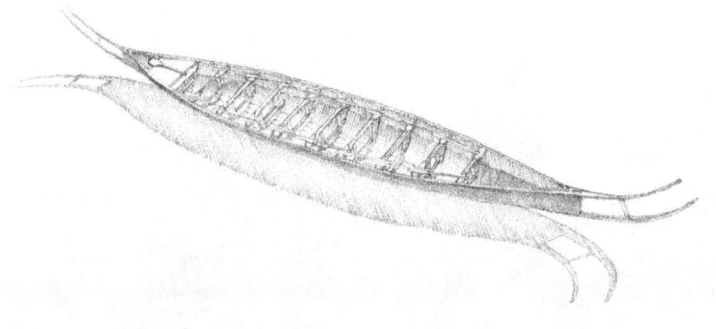

TOPOGRAPHIC PILGRIMAGES

LAIKA

Over 50 years
since Laika's heartbeat has been heard

Orbiting 1,031 miles above earth
in a silver sphere

Man's best friend   first in space   a lonely pinprick of light
hurling through heavens

Faithfully awaiting
her master's call

APOLLO

Liftoff
Sealed inside service modules
three stories of liquid light
counting down
2 ignition
launchpad severing umbilical cords
Saturn V
blasting astronauts weightless

Falling faster
than any relative sense of motion
toward the debris-shattered face of moon

The Dark Side
Men flying alone into radio blackouts
over moon's dark side
deliberately extinguishing cabin lights
piloting spacecraft into stars uninterrupted by sky

Landing
3000 feet into descent
program alarms sounding   guidance system down
coming in long   low on fuel
LM's shadow cast on radial curtains of dust

Commander
feeling his way down
over
craters the size of inverted football domes
boulder fields larger than semi-trucks

Eagle landing
Tranquility Base
the lunar module's
one two-hundredth of an inch thick skin
separating man   moon

Lunar Ascent
A felt-tipped pen
shoved into severed arming breaker
igniting engines lifting *Apollo 11* off lunar surface
in the aluminum foil of fire
ascending through blinding lunar light
reflecting dusty scent of *wet ashes* tracked into cabin
trilateral window's framing falling stars   stripes

Return
Pulled back from the apogee of black
molten tears
streaking through blue flame
human beings
strapped inside ionized ablations   shooting stars

Apollo 18
Apollo 18 lies on its side
a thunderbolt broken into four segments
300 feet of frozen thrust
engineered to rain heaven
upon earth
unignited
corroding back into a country of voyeurs
lost in cyberspace

GEORGE WASHINGTON

Wrinkled George Washington
looks out of his window
on a one dollar bill   the man
who refused to be king

Larger than he used to be   worth less
the founding father   frozen   diversified   liquefied
counterfeited   robbed

Financing architects   mercenaries
philanthropists   television evangelists
he has sent men to the moon and Guantanamo Bay

Begged   borrowed   bartered   bought and sold
passed from the hands of coal miners   steel makers   pimps
successors who took him off the gold standard   printed him at will

George W. infiltrated
with holographic security strips   shipped to foreign shores
overthrowing sovereign nations   finalizing deals
with mass murderers

Embezzled   exchanged   burned   buried   gambled
away   folded in half   hung from g-strings

The Virginia Gentleman
hoarded   hungered for   rolled up
used to snort cocaine
lost   found   given away

Money talks
America doesn't listen

Novus Ordo Seclorum   In God we trust   Legal tender

Another devalued   defaced   dead president
presiding over a country
with no hard currency

TRENTON, 2009

Thunder volleys through forest at dawn
a running battle with Winter
bare trees thrusting bayonets through black powder
lightning's flintlock flash
charging over torsos of trunks

Struggling to lift gangrenous limbs
off field's fermenting leaves

The grapeshot of hail
forcing seasoned soldiers
to retreat into hybrid cars

FLYING OVER THE MIDWEST

Great Plains
plowed into flags:

Fields of wheat
waving stars and stripes
over buffalo skulls

Crop circles appearing in farmland:
phases of moon   fallen planets   clocks   compasses

Bull's-eyes

DANCING ON THE CHARLES BRIDGE

A blade of grass moving counter-clockwise
over eight-year-old face
striking sunset in Prague's cobblestone sky
Tyn's metronome of spires ticking off notes

Freezing earth's astronomical axis
where father and daughter
always swing with the saints
marching across the Charles Bridge

HEMINGWAY'S SUITCASE

A coffee table
in Borges' study
turned out to be Hemingway's suitcase
stolen from a train compartment at the Gare de Lyon, 1922

The Argentinian writer
purchased the piece of luggage
from a former porter
in a Paris flea market
for the price of a good Bordeaux

After reading the paper contents of the case
Señor Borges threw the American's prose into the Seine
convinced fiction
could no longer be real

ZONA ROJO

Dawn in Guadalajara

Old women sweeping dirt courtyards
open doorways welcoming rain

Seventeen-year-old girls
lining tree-busted streets:

Paper flowers   carnitas for twenty-five American dollars

Rolls of toilet tissue   condoms
rooms with naked windows
bed sheets surrendering wind

Crouching down on hands and knees
burying heads in pillows

Never kissing customers on lips

FALLING

Into the mist of the Northeast Ridge
into avalanches of cloud

Words wrapped in a red handkerchief
broken rope around waist

Facedown frozen in gravel
the jet stream howling mountain

*The margin of strength
when men are at great heights is small*

Less than finite   says Hartshorne
more than *The Yellow Band* of desire

You fell backwards
into your *Alptraum*   the arms of friends
forty feet of weightlessness
because mind was not tied to cliff

Why risk another climber's life
to cover a marble body with stones?

Let the goraks have their souvenir wristwatches   goggles

Who needs Somervell's camera
to prove whether or not the summit
was ever within reach?

SKATEBOARDING IN NUREMBERG

A blitzkrieg
of skateboarding shock troops
catching air in Speer's stadium

A Stuka dive
across Hitler's balcony back in time:

10,000 banners flying
spotlights projecting swastikas
vectoring clouds

Grandchildren of the Third Reich
grinding down granite steps into 360s

Iron crosses on black caps

SWEET DESTINY

Heinrich Stollwerck's
5-cylinder mill   fondant boiler

Stainless steel plaque
read: *Reichspatent #10436*

Exploded May 15, 1915   Cologne, Germany

Killed its inventor
with chocolate

BERLIN, 1987

05:00   Frankfurt Bahnhof:

Men drinking beer
on their way to work

Rolling through farmland
towards Silvesterabend on the Spree

Helmstedt   Deutsche Demokratische Republik
East German soldiers boarding train cars:

Green coats   dogs   AK-47s
shouting   *Pass bitte!*
Cities still frozen by air raids

Towering smokestacks aspirating large blocks
of crumbling brick apartments

Apparitions shuffling down streets in black suits
no color except for propaganda

Whistling past signposts
at speeds wiping villages off maps

Locomotive outflanking Soviet Army bases
third-class students yawning democracy
pointing to rows of rusting artillery tanks   whispering to me
This is the evil empire your president fears

15:00   armed escorts
exiting at Potsdam   Sanssouci Palace
vanishing behind barbed-wire gardens

Watchtowers watching
train tracks suture stitching slashed /earth

16:00   next stop: Zoo Station
Kaiser Wilhelm's bombed-out church steeple
foaming fireworks over the Ku'damm's cabaret of lights   graffiti-jazz

JFK dead wrong—Ich bin nicht *ein Berliner*

We are Berlin
airlifting
Checkpoint Charlie   Coca-Cola—Cold War
U-bahn moaning beneath Tiergarten's numbered trees

Reichstag rising out of blasted teacups   beer steins   bullet holes

Warning!
You are leaving the American sector
Entering the Russian zone

Stalinallee Stasi goose-stepping through Brandenburg Gate
concrete bunkers where our father sleeps
dreaming: triumphant arches   great domes   topography of terrors

Representatives of the free world
shouting   *Tear down this wall!*

SAVIGNYPLATZ (BERLIN, 2007)

Climbing out of Savignyplatz

Linden tree of sound
candlelit conversations   bottle breaking
bursts of laughter

Knocking on balcony doorways
late night footsteps   rolling over cobblestone street   a car

In a neighborhood built on buried voices
the approaching thunder of S-Bahn
comforting a metropolis that cannot sleep

POTSDAMER PLATZ PIGEONS

Pigeons
in Potsdamer Platz
threaded sticks   strands of hair
in war-torn brick buildings
wove nests of architectural atonement

INTIMATE GEOGRAPHY

How do I
an American   go home
after walking through the blue gate of Babylon
climbing 509 steps up Kölner Dom?

How do I disembark?
Declare myself a citizen of one country
after eating salmon from Ramsauer Ache
its shade   its taste   a color   no word in English

How do I stroll
from marble streets softened by centuries of footsteps
onto concrete?

Who in my hometown
will call me over to a car trunk
to feel for fingerprints
in 300-year-old brick?

Who will drive me across unguarded borders
to taste Monschau mustard?
To heal my eyes in Heilbrünnl's fountain?

FIRENZA

I left my suitcase in Florence
because it was large
and I did not know how to travel

I like to think
an Italian boy is wearing the button-down shirt
left inside the luggage

I close my eyes
and he's pulling a pack of cigarettes from the front pocket
sleeves slapping wind wordless

The Palazzo Vecchio
stamping its imprimatur
on the color of cloth

It is possible in this inferno of city
to live two separate lives

PERSONAL GEOGRAPHY

PRAYER OF FORGIVENESS

Forgive us for compassion
anathema to credo
for courage to live the *kingdom*
excommunicated from Christianity

Forgive us for feeding the poor
only to be banished to medieval texts
hands folded by prayer

Forgive us for youth sacrificed on altars
of false prophets   pompous presbyters
for incantations of iconoclastic blasphemy
in the face of infallible hypocrisy

Forgive us for casting the monstrance of pious masturbation
into stained glass
for becoming acolytes in *the priesthood of all believers*

Forgive us for love before Canon Law and prophylactic pontifications
for monogamy before ecclesiastical ejaculations
cloaked in celibacy and the robotic worship of the laity

Forgive us for leaving the womb of Holy Mother Church
only to find faith reborn in unbelievers
redemption in the unprofessed magesterium of an unnameable God

After all these years of unconsecrated anger
accept the rock that sealed our hearts

GONE

Gone
as all gods go:

No fractal bolts of lightning
flooding eyes with thunder's ritual refrain

I walk alone among crippled arches   broken obelisks
seeking metamorphosis
not movement

RUMI'S MIRROR

A month
in meditation   fasting

Shattered
by the blonde prayer-beaded sun
bouncing off her black Mercedes

Top down

MATHEMATICAL PROOF

The weed whacker's wail
diving beneath a thunderclap of scissor-stabbed water

Light calculating its mathematical proof for wind's existence
on the body of a woman
swimming into pool's deep end

SEVEN CAVES

A shaman paints his face white
paddles out through shore break

Parting waves drawn by currents
into the seven caves of La Jolla

Seagulls singing from muddy lofts
Garibaldi's orange flame the only inextinguishable light
flickering in dark water

SILENCE

At night ocean kneels on a mosaic of stones
does not mourn the shroud
Winter swept away

Birds walk barefoot on rock
read hieroglyphics of wind with wings

Tangled cages rust into the afterbirth of kelp:

Remnants of glass worn into submission by sea

Moonlight curls up inside crashing waves
christening algorithms of shadow and shore

Creates a moment between contractions
when everything in the universe is

Silence

PROJECTILE POINT

From bowstring
over canyons bruised by cloud

Through bighorn sheep
brooming monzonite quartz

The arrow shooting out of centuries of sand-swamped riverbeds
into human hands again

INDIAN ROCK

Evening's evaporating light releases whales
beached inside mammoth boulders

Stirs bifurcated tide pools   eye lashing anemones   seagrass

Flips through manuscripts of gold slate
teeming manta rays   monkfish

Lifts painted faces from bleached rock

WHEN OCEANS HAD FISH

Remember when oceans had fish?

Before stingrays lay in sandstone
hammerhead sharks prowling waves of alluvial plains
breaking bottlenose dolphins?

Before the Subtropical Convergence Zone
contaminated seven seas
and the last grey whale migrated into 2 KBs of digital memory?

Before the struggle between
man-made tsunamis   marlin   beast?

BLUE SCREEN

Turn off the cell phone
let the blue screen go black

Remember Saturday's sound
before Xboxes?

Chattering birds laughing so loudly outside sleeping houses
they flew into dreams?

Walk away from the machine
open a door
the sparrows haven't deleted their song

DOORWAYS

If laurel sumac
thrives in fire's aftermath

Ghost-dancing Joshua trees
propagate in white ponchos of snow

If astronauts can leap for joy in 250 degrees of sun
blasting black daylight

There must be doorways
opening into coruscating seas
where travelers search for gravity
in the space splashing around them

X-RAYS

Why should I be surprised
to find a tumor
in the frontal lobe of Texas?

I thought I encountered it all:

Needle pricking cholla
releasing petrified fish onto dry lakes

Snake biting sun rattling beneath rocks

Barium stained tarantulas
crawling across plates of obsidian night

Surprise is an unaffordable luxury
in the trauma room of America

The real work begins
after the x-rays have been read

When silver
is extracted from film

CARVING A PUMPKIN

Scooping
orange matter
from pumpkin cranium

Candlelight carving triangular eyes
summoning the
severed head
to life

TRANSFIGURATION
In the spirit of Walt Whitman

We lie within the warmth of each other's bodies
candlelight in paper lanterns
purple lesions darkening flesh:
fingerprints of an internal flame

There is no word in scripture
for the sacrament of my skin touching yours
we sleep together at this station of the cross

Sometimes your silence awakens me
I watch you transfigured by the white host of moon
the braille of your bones betrays a soul close to the surface now

An apparition of the gay Christ
shrouded in hospital sheets
how few disciples see you have come again

WALKING CLOSE TO CLIFFS

Walking close to cliffs
knowing they fall

It's comforting to touch time
told in laminated layers of sandstone

The second hand of human history
barely scratching 46 million years
angling from beach to bluff

The line of human life in landslides stacked on shore

The cool spray of Pleistocene ocean
bubbling brown slab

One rock among many
sheared out of sedimentary veneer
sorted by sea

PARROT STREET

What lies buried beneath Parrot Street
pushing up sidewalk in front of tract housing?

What happened to the fossilized footprint
found walking in Pliocene waves of sandstone
now entombed by Interstate 805
or the Vietcong belt buckle
our neighbor brought back from Nam?

30 years after ivy caught the left-field fly
hit over our family's television antenna
landsliding earth
knocked the ball into backyard again:
the only homerun

Nothing remaining to mark the concrete
genuflecting into asphalt
where Mr. Jones pulled out of the American dream never to return again

Cars rush over a manhole cover
preserving the signatures of children
swept from faces on welcome mats that porches no longer recall

What lies beneath Parrot Street
under the pendulum of empty swings
swaying sandboxes?

What conversations have been hushed by hissing high-tension wires?

CONSTRUCTION SITE

Quiet calls the hawk
over sleeping contruction sites
searching frozen trucks   dozers for food

Half-finished houses
sit in acetylene sun
wind shredding surveyor flags

Coyotes stand at attention on naked medians

Blocks of vacant lots   PVC pipe protrudes from graded earth:

Waving hands
sawed off before they could signal—   *Help!*

Plastic wrappers
scratch cement slabs

In the deserted distance a nail-gun shoots silence

SAN DIEGO

They say San Diego has one season
when Fall is a fire ring of Santa Ana winds tearing through trees

When Winter frost gathers in avocado groves
the maze of San Dieguito riverbed
predicting flood

When Spring is a firestorm of poppies
ranunculus running in formation down Carlsbad hills
they say San Diego has one season

Summer evaporation emptying reservoirs
automatic sprinklers dancing the tango on golf courses
from desert to coast

JESUS WAS A WOMAN

Jesus was a woman
wrapped in a veil of tears

Turning water into wine

Loving an enemy
who could not love himself
Body broken
hands washed in blood

Jesus was a woman
taken away by the sins of the world
nailed to the cross of man

Grant her peace

INCANDESCENT

Looking at me
from an incandescent world

Constellations of starfish
burning from four fathoms of eyes

Windy currents
running hands through hair

Eyelashes of light
brushing against skin

So close I can't read her lips
without fog clouding her face

FLOATING

Beneath our boat
a forest of kelp
rising from ocean floor

Soaring
above seaweed's calligraphy of reason   the Morse-code current
tapping its fingers against hull

A sea of voices in extremis
no foghorn listening

One sun broken
into a thousand pixels of light

I am other than these beaded thoughts of air
bursting sky   floating speechless

Ozone blue
winking into black

The center of earth's eye

AFTER THE WITCH CREEK FIRE

Plagiobothrys:
Popcorn flower
blisters out of burn area
minute white blades
hovering

Above salverform silence
profoundly burned landscape

The cormorant's amplified wing clap
thundering across Lake Hodges

WILD
For Anne Swanke

Wild wind
shaking down sagebrush

Kicking soil into dust storms
combing grass into semaphores

Sweeping down sky
to steal the life of a single leaf

GEOPOLITICS

BUTTERFLY STORM *(VANESSA CARDUI)*

Vanessa cardui
swarming in over coyote grey ocean

Illegal aliens
uncontested except for windshields

Abandoned to the bureaucracy of breeze

CANYON SIN NOMBRE

There were signs
leading away from Canyon Sin Nombre
the Kumeyaay people could have read:

Deer tracks treading over dry creeks   a horseshoe in Box Canyon

Mine shafts erupting lava flows of highway
driving automobiles into the wash of sprawling ghost towns

EL NIÑO

After El Niño
left the beach without fascia—
rock beat against stone in receding waves
mounds of decomposing kelp broke:
Styrofoam-white on razor shore

The ocean heaved
plastic forks   spoons   anonymous cans offering saltwater
debrided canisters and tubes

Sunglasses staring blindly out of sand
surfboard fins circling discarded tampons

Fishing tackle
reeling in emasculated straws
a child's decapitated doll

In the riptide of rubbish:
a single white shoe
immaculately preserved by sea's centrifuge
as if it had never been worn

POETRY FOR CROWS

It is madness to write poetry in cities over
run by crows

Meta
phor pecked a
part as
if it were bare
bone fact

Gangs of scavengers
happily haggling
over herniated garbage
bags

WALKING THROUGH DACHAU

No sign of smoke
hanging over crematorium

No soldiers guarding empty barracks

No trains breaking   miles of muted tracks

An act of violence to claim the camp liberated
when no one can walk anywhere within wire
without stepping on screaming mouths of leaves

INVASION

Television
casting
shadows of war
on the sleeping infant's face

PRESIDENT CLINTON'S CIGAR

While sentinels sat inside mountains of reinforced steel
plotting missile strikes
on pharmaceutical amusement parks

The country reduced to ashes by a cigar
maneuvered between the labia of global corporations:

Smoke rings masking the neocons' hostile takeover

GROUND ZERO

People will ask where you were today
when Todd Kulik went to work for Morgan Stanley
Tower II   World Trade Center

Tell them you woke up on a street meaning *orphan* in Spanish
three miles from the mosque
where Nawaf al-Hazmi   Khalid al-Mihdhar
took their shoes off   faced Mecca:

The faithful called to blood-stained prayer rugs
in the name of a mirage

People will ask where you were
when Tower I erupted jet fuel spreadsheets   for martyrs
in business suits
burning from minarets to earth

Tell them you were two years old
Sufi dancing in front of television set
when a voice within the stairwell of Todd K.
louder than management's instructions to remain at desks
talked him down 70 stories into sunlight
United Airlines   Flight 175   slamming building above him

People will ask where you were
when the World Trade Center fell into smoldering steel
clouds of pulverized concrete
smothering survivors in white vernix

Tell them because someday they will ask
tell them you looked into the blue silence of heaven
no aluminum wings cauterizing sky
shock waves rippling across country

KOENIG'S SPHERE

No one recognized
Koenig's bronze eye
staring out of steel at Ground Zero

Ignorant rescue workers cut through sclera
torching the globe

DUMBING DOWN

When the loan is larger than the market value of a home
when the metallic worth of a penny is greater
than its face value

When African Americans
call themselves *niggers*

When more men are held in prisons
than study in schools

When smart bombs
cost more to construct than bridges they destroy
thN w'r nt as smrt as we tnk w'r

THE SIXTH YEAR

In the sixth year of the war on terror:
passengers removing shoes   boarding planes
reading sports pages   watching reality TV
country cowering in spider holes   AWOL   wireless world
texting English into oblivion

In the sixth year of the war on terror:
commuters in SUVs roaming the earth   searching for parking spaces
talking to themselves
believing   *work makes men free*
ordering F-18 fighter pilots
to Camp Pendleton for retraining   because   *every Marine is a rifleman*

German artist Roger Rigorth chained to an INS van in April
for the crime of landing at LAX with a passport

In the sixth year of the war on terror:
the police state
data-mining democracy   outsourcing torture
making Americans victims of identity theft
the wound at Ground Zero
contaminating country   flooding New Orleans
with trailer parks from gulf to rising sea

In the sixth year of the war on terror:
killing the US Army with friendly fire   abandoning soldiers
hemorrhaging purple hearts in hospital waiting rooms

Still searching for weapons of mass destruction
Green zone   shrinking

Global warming   global warming!

FLYING FLAGS

Free countries
don't pledge allegiance to nylon stars

Don't require
honest men to swear on Bibles

Free countries
don't fly flags from suit lapels   used car lots

Free countries
burn flags not people

THE ASSASSINATION OF BENAZIR BHUTTO

What looks like breeze
surging through eucalyptus leaves
is the concussion of a child's scream
carried halfway round earth

What appears to be rain
parachuting into pools swimming with clouds
is actually a mother's tears

What is forecast as thunder
in sunny Rancho Bernardo
is the secondary fragmentation from a bomb blast
two continents away

STAUFFENBERG'S EYE

A blind Bedouin
stumbled upon Count Stauffenberg's eye
lost where the Wehrmacht soldier fell wounded
North Africa   World War II

Today it looks out of sun-strafed face
watching American-made ordnance
dismember Palestinian children on Al Jazeera TV

It stares at the strange man in mirrors
knowing there will never be another opportunity
to kill the tyrant arisen from ashes
when yellow stars are beat into swastikas
and every continent has its Führer

THE EIGHTH YEAR

In the eighth year of the war on terror:
alarms going off   houses lighting up
husbands kissing wives

Armchair warriors commuting to cubicles in the Sunshine State
working nine to five
shooting Hellfire missiles at Pashtun villages with joysticks

Osama bin Laden walking   Obama talking
don't ask   don't tell
no tribunal for the Vice President of Torture
just cable news game shows
waterboarding US soldiers for profit

Wall Street rising   Main Street crashing
cash for clunkers   bailouts for bankers
25-year-old Marines recycled   reused   going green

In the eighth year of the war on terror:
no virgins for suicide bombers   no second coming
just virtual men   women   children smiling facebooks

The titanic ship of state
a lonely iceberg run aground by Captains of Industry

Drunken passengers
twittering on the edge of extinction

LEADING ECONOMIC INDICATOR

Old enough to be a grandfather

The rebooted
small businessman is bagging
canned goods   fronting merchandise

Mopping up spilled milk
on Aisle 9

SEEING

I see you standing in traffic
hood of a sweatshirt
pulling down
your face

In another time:
invoking ancestral spirits
because no one eats and drinks
from the same plate
in this divided
land

In another place:
a monk meditating on the wounds of Christ
the forsaken savior's clothing
soiled by charity's washed hands

I see you   I see the man   maybe a woman
blurred by rearview mirror

Feel the dirt beneath fingernails
digging deeper
into impossible earth

Our eyes never meet but I see you watching me
I am turning   turning away
from myself

POLITICAL FETISH

If big business is in bed with small government
trickle-down economics
is a face of bukkake for the shrinking middle class

Call me a slacker
but it's the only form of protest left

If cost of living ≠ mean family income
then *working poor*
is a euphemism for slavery

As long as *tea-bagging* capitalists
don't have balls to admit they are into bondage

Call me a socialist pig
but I won't be sold on the free market
by the republic of organized crime

If cell phones are the eyes and ears of the NSA
Uncle Sam is a Peeping Tom

Call me a tree-hugging atheist
but collecting people's dirty laundry doesn't turn me on

If the constitution is a rag
for presidents to wipe away wet dreams

Washington might as well be blowing British Petroleum
or giving handjobs to the Red Army in Tiananmen Square

Call me an exsanguinated liberal
but auto-erotically asphyxiating habeas corpus
smothers us all

If Lady Liberty is a dominatrix
screwing sovereign nations into submission
with strap-ons and watersports

Call me un-American
but boot-licking sadomasochism isn't patriotic
it's pornography

If wearing a uniform is the only way
for young adults to make a living
our country is a police state

Handcuffs and leather may get some people off
but whatever happened to making love?

BOARDING A SINKING SHIP

Why board a sinking ship?

The first 300 passengers to purchase a ticket
receive discounts on future cruises

Firing flare guns is against the law in suburban backyards
once life jackets are issued everybody looks the same

Blended icebergs make frosty margaritas
playing roulette with life makes it sensible to lose shirts in cabin casinos

Orchestras play peak performances before slipping beneath waves
lifeboats lower passengers into more intimate depths
women and children come first
it might be nice to be rescued

Sharks are expected in water
seafood is fresher
if you've got to go under at least there's comfort knowing
the captain will go down with his ship

The ocean doesn't discriminate
based on gender   color   religious affiliation   class
it receives all passengers equally

FEAST OF FORGETTING

Bin Laden was shot today,
A high-ranking Marine smiles,
*They wrapped his torso in bacon before tossing it
into a sea of bloodsucking bottom-dwellers*

In Los Angeles a child is going to bed hungry
the open sore of street is gangrenous

Across town
bloated suits sit down to gorge themselves on gourmet meals
sizzling short sales   fat trimmed from corpses
still warm from Afghanistan

Anyone who has been outside the meat locker knows
they are serving up the past medium rare

Slaughter isn't cheap—
butchers must be paid their fair market share
of amputated limbs from body farms
99% of hides hanging from hooks
over factory floors

The rest of LA is left to lick pink slime
from the mouths of returning soldiers—
swig human waste from water faucets

The orgy of knives and forks
must go on stabbing choice cuts
into gristle

Most mad cows
in hunger's belly inflated metropolis
would kill for a slice of freezer-burned gristle
scarf down bowls of bloodshot eyes mocking the gluttony of ignorance
no one would feed dogs

The drunken desperation to forget
drink and forget the city is eating its own flesh

Stuffing mouths so full no one can speak for themselves
deliriously swallowing tongues

BLOOD ON LATEX

Fetus taken
feet first from womb

Metzenbaum scissors
thrust into brain

Cerebral cortex suctioned from skull
blood on latex gloves

STRIKING A CHILD

A child is struck by his father
knocking wind
from words

Witnesses
scattering shadows
bystanders
blinking blind eyes

Conversations
picked up where they were kicked to ground

The seeing
no longer believing

Ordering desserts
asking waiters for checks

Crêpe suzettes   ladyfingers
withering into Dresden porcelain

ACCIDENT SCENE

70 miles per hour cigarette exploding
asphalt

Slashing straight line
into dashes   dots

Headlights brushing embedded glass:

Rush hour's *Starry Night*

WMD

In countries
where people read

A writer
would rot in prison
for burning his president in prose
in the land that manufactured *Don't Ask, Don't Tell*
remote-controlled drones

The poet
faces a new weapon
in the history of dictatorships:
he is ignored

NOTES

p. 53 The Yellow Band: a distinct sedimentary feature on Mount Everest
Alptraum: a German word for nightmare.
Somervell: Theodore Howard Somervell was a mountaineer. He was present on the second British Expedition to Mount Everest during which George Mallory and Andrew Irvine disappeared. Somervell lent his camera to Mallory on Mallory's third attempt to summit Everest. George Mallory was never seen again.

p. 56 Silvesterabend on the Spree: New Year's Eve on the Spree River (which runs through Berlin).

p. 61 Heilbrünnl's fountain: a church fountain in the Bavarian town of Heilbrünnl said to heal ailments of the eyes.

p. 91 Vanessa cardui: the Painted Lady Butterfly.

ACKNOWLEDGMENTS

The poems in this collection were previously published in the following magazines, newspapers, anthologies, and web sites: The University of San Diego's Vista newspaper, Erratica, Poetry Conspiracy, Coast Highway Review, Magee Park Anthology, San Diego Magazine, Mira Costa College's Tidepools Anthology, Eating Her Wedding Dress, San Diego City College's City Works, Coast News, San Diego Annual, Today's Alternative News, Gravity and Nomadism, www.contemporaryworldpoetry.com and mahmag.org.

Vielen Dank to Roger Rigorth for generously contributing his illustrations and photography to this book. May Der Flow be with you, Captain!

I wish to thank James Allen, Linda Brown, Joe Fuhrman, Dr. Sam Hamod, Shadab Zeest Hashmi, Marilyn Heidrick, Tim Herr, the Hörken's family, Karen Kenyon, Karolin Mangold, G. McFadden, the Magee Park poetry community, Donald Prisby, Dr. Nicholas Reveles, Charlotte Rose, R. T. Sedgwick, Lilian Thoma, Claudia Schlee, Tender Art, Marla Vencil, John Watt, and Jon Wesick, for the wisdom, encouragement, and inspiration which enabled me to find my poetic voice.

A big thanks to Anna Penigina (www.annatica.com), Mily Dahlke, and William Wilson for their expertise with InDesign layout.

I would also like to thank everyone at Ragged Sky Press for being the catalyst for this project. I am especially indebted to my editors Ellen Foos and Arlene Weiner for their hard work and professional feedback. Thanks for bringing out the best in my poetry!

Many thanks to Meg, Greta, and my family for the über-love and support they have given me over the years to develop as a poet. This is for you!

www.ingramcontent.com/pod-product-compliance
Lightning Source LLC
Chambersburg PA
CBHW020941090426
42736CB00010B/1223